HELLO, GEORGE WASHINGTON!

BY JANICE HOLLAND

ABINGDON PRESS
New York · Nashville
COPYRIGHT © 1958 BY ABINGDON PRESS
ALL RIGHTS RESERVED · LITHOGRAPHED IN THE U.S.A.
A

HELLO, GEORGE WASHINGTON!

A thin sheet of ice covered the Potomac River one February morning long ago in Virginia. On the river's bank, a curl of blue smoke rose from the chimney of a snug brick house.

Inside the house was a baby, newly born. The baby's parents, Augustine and Mary Washington, smiled. "Hello, George!" said Augustine to his new son. "Hello, George Washington!"

As soon as George Washington could walk, he followed his father around the big farm where they lived. Most of all, George loved to visit the stables and see the beautiful horses.

George often begged his father to take him for a ride, but Augustine Washington would shake his head. "You're too little now," he would say.

At last the day came when George's father lifted him up into the saddle, and then mounted behind. How far away the ground looked as George and his father rode together over the fields!

FERRY FARM

When George was six years old, his family moved to a farm on the Rappahannock River. It was called Ferry Farm because a ferryboat took people back and forth across the river near the house.

Shouting teamsters rode across in their heavy wagons. Fine gentlemen rode across in their handsome coaches. George Washington rode across on his own two feet.

On the other side of the river was a school for boys. At this school, George learned to read and write and

do arithmetic. Later, he learned some rules for good manners. One of them was: "In the presence of others, sing not to yourself with a humming noise, nor drum with your fingers or feet."

When George was eleven years old, his father died. Ferry Farm did not seem the same after that. Still, George and his three brothers had good times together. They swam in the Rappahannock River. They rode horseback. They climbed trees and romped in the hayloft.

Page 5

HOLD ON, GEORGE!

George's favorite sport was horseback riding.

Early one morning, George and some other boys were visiting Mrs. Washington's stables. Her favorite sorrel colt was galloping about the yard. This colt was wild. No one had ever been able to ride him.

Suddenly George asked his friends to hold the colt while he mounted. When they let go, the colt sprang into the air, twisting and kicking.

The colt reared wildly. George tightened his knees against the horse's sides. He would not give up. The horse plunged more wildly. *He* would not give up. After one last great leap, the colt fell dead.

At that moment the breakfast bell rang. Frightened and silent, the boys took their seats at the table. Mrs. Washington began to question them.

"Did you see my colts this morning?" she asked.

George's corn bread stuck in his throat.

Then his mother said, "And how is my favorite, the sorrel?"

George swallowed hard. "The sorrel is dead, Madam."

Slowly, George told the whole story. When he had finished, his mother was silent for a moment. Then she said, "I am sorry to have lost my colt, but I am glad to have a son who always speaks the truth."

MOUNT VERNON

After losing her colt, Mrs. Washington knew that George needed a man to take his father's place. George admired his older half-brother, Lawrence. More and more often he was sent to visit Lawrence. Lawrence lived at Mount Vernon. Mount Vernon stood on a green hill, high above the Potomac River.

Life at Mount Vernon was gay. Lawrence and his wife, Anne, gave many parties. George was not used to parties. He could not forget his big hands and feet.

George decided, however, that he must learn the ways of Mount Vernon. He studied dancing. Soon he began to like parties. Lawrence's friends liked George.

INDIANS!

One of Lawrence's friends was Lord Fairfax. He owned land in western Virginia. When George was sixteen years old, he was invited to help survey, or measure, Lord Fairfax's land.

George had always lived in a good house, and slept in clean feather beds. Now he was leaving home to camp on the ground in the wild forests.

The trip was a rainy one. One river was so flooded that no one could cross it. George and his friends had to wait at a trading post until the waters went down.

Soon a war party of thirty Indians came to the post. George's spine tingled. These were the first Indian braves he had ever seen. They were wet and cold.

After the Indians had dried themselves, they began to feel gay. They stretched a skin over a kettle to make a drum. They filled some gourds with shot to make them rattle. They built a great fire, and around it they danced a war dance. They made George laugh.

In spite of the hardships, George loved the wilderness. He never forgot his first adventures there.

DANGER, BEWARE!

When George was twenty years old, his half-brother Lawrence died. George became the master of Mount Vernon.

The next year, George offered to go on a long and dangerous journey for the British government. Christopher Gist, an expert scout, went with him. The two men traveled through frozen woods and crossed many ice-choked rivers.

One day, after walking many miles, Washington and Gist decided to stop and rest. At that moment, their Indian guide turned his gun upon them and fired at close range.

"Are you shot?" Washington called out.

"No, but where is the Indian?" Gist answered.

Both men hurried forward. They found the Indian behind a large tree, loading his rifle again. They seized him at once.

"We must kill him," said Gist.

"No," said George Washington. "Enemies have told him to do this." He knew, however, that the Indian could not be trusted. He and Gist watched for a chance to slip away. Tired as they were, the two men walked all that night and all the next day to escape the Indian. After many adventures, they reached their homes again.

MORE INDIANS

Before long, the French and Indians were at war with the British. General Braddock came from Britain to lead the fight against the French and Indians. He asked George Washington to be one of his officers.

Braddock's army marched proudly into the wilderness. The General, however, had never fought Indians. The bright red coats of his soldiers made good targets in the dark green forests.

In the first big battle, the General was killed. Though George Washington had been ill, he took Braddock's place at the head of the troops.

Washington rode into the thick of the fight. Two horses were shot from under him, and four bullets cut his clothing. He tried to rally his men, but in spite of his bravery, the battle was lost.

News of the terrible defeat raced through the colonies. With it went word of the brave young George Washington, who had tried so hard to win. Soon he was given command of all the Virginia troops.

For three years, George Washington lived on the frontier. He tried to protect the settlers who were attacked by Indians, but many were murdered. Washington grew homesick for Mount Vernon. Yet he did not leave until the Virginia frontier was safe.

HELLO, MARTHA CUSTIS!

When, at last, Washington returned home, the most important people in the Colony of Virginia gathered for a wedding. It was a bright day in January. The bride was Martha Custis, the richest widow in Virginia. The groom was George Washington, the most famous young officer in the Colony.

In February, George and Martha went to Williamsburg. Martha's children, Jackie and Patsy Custis, went with them. Williamsburg was the capital of Virginia. George had been elected to help govern the Colony.

Williamsburg was gay with balls and parties. It was a happy time for the Washingtons.

Page 17

When spring came, George and Martha, Jackie and Patsy, hurried to Mount Vernon. It was time to plant the crops.

How Washington loved his home! Every day he rode over his fields. He tried new crops and new ways of planting.

Mount Vernon hummed with work. George loved to take Jackie and Patsy with him when he visited his plantation shops. The children liked the slosh-closh-plosh of the churn, and the clang-dang-bang of the blacksmith's hammer.

WAR!

Page 18

One day, George Washington sadly said good-by to his family. There was trouble between the American colonists and their British king. British soldiers had already fired upon some Americans in Boston. George Washington was going to Philadelphia to meet with other leaders from the thirteen colonies.

At this meeting, the Americans chose George Washington to lead their armies against the British troops. The Americans were not ready for war. Washington's soldiers were ragged and hungry. They walked with bleeding feet through the winter snows.

Washington looked at his "ragged boys" and wondered how they could ever win the war. But he would not give up, even in the dark, cold days at Valley Forge.

Though the British had gay uniforms, Washington and his "ragged boys" had courage. They fought on and on. After six years, the British at last surrendered to George Washington. The Americans were free! They called their country the United States of America.

George Washington accepted no payment for all his years as General of the American armies. To serve his country was an honor. He wanted no other reward.

VISITORS, VISITORS, VISITORS!

George Washington was now the most famous man in America. People from far and near came to Mount Vernon. They wanted to meet the great General.

Washington was kind to them all. No one was turned away without food and drink. There were so many visitors that Washington wrote, "A hundred cows do not supply enough butter for my household."

At another meeting in Philadelphia, George Washington helped to set up a government for the new country, the United States of America. People all over the country wanted him to be its first President.

Washington had hoped to spend the rest of his life at Mount Vernon, but when he was asked to become President, he put duty first. Amid the waving of flags, the playing of bands, and the cheers of his fellow citizens, he traveled to New York. There he was inaugurated as the first President of the United States.

DUTY, DUTY, DUTY!

HELLO, U.S.A.!

Not long after George Washington became President, Congress decided to build a new city. This city was to be the capital of the United States of America. Congress decided to call the city "Washington," and to build it on the Potomac River. President Washington was asked to choose the place.

George Washington mounted his horse. He rode nearly two hundred miles along the Potomac. He finally decided to build the capital city just twelve miles above Mount Vernon.

While he was President, George Washington visited every state in the new United States of America. He stopped his coach to talk with farmers by the roadside. He walked through the streets of cities, looking carefully at everything.

For George Washington wanted America's farms to have good harvests, and her factories to make fine cloth. To be a good President, he must learn as much as possible about his country and its people.

Merchants, workers and farmers welcomed Washington wherever he went. Often, cheering crowds lined the streets. When the citizens saw their beloved President, they felt proud and happy to belong to the new country, the United States of America.

GOOD-BY, GEORGE WASHINGTON!

After eight years as President and First Lady, George and Martha Washington returned to Mount Vernon. It seemed more beautiful than ever. Martha's granddaughter, Nellie Custis, and her friends filled the house with laughter.

Washington wanted no praise from his fellow citizens, but they could not forget all that he had done. Many of them visited him at Mount Vernon. He never talked about his victories, nor the great honors he had won. To himself, he was only a Virginia farmer. To all other Americans, he was ". . . first in war, first in peace, and first in the hearts of his countrymen."